영어 필기체
100일 기적의 노트

KB191576

기획 · 구성 펜앤페이퍼(Pen&Paper)

읽는 일과 쓰는 일을 하는 출판기획 모임입니다.
책읽기의 즐거움과 손글씨 감성을 함께 느낄 수 있는 책들을 기획하고 있습니다.
만든 책으로는《영어 필기체 10일 완성 노트》《음악이 있는 팝송 영어 필사》
《어린 왕자 영어 필기체 100일 필사 노트》등이 있습니다.

감수 이지(Izzie)

미국 보스턴에 있는 버클리 음대를 졸업하고, 뉴욕과 LA에서 음악과 관련된 일을 오랫동안 했습니다.
지금은 우리나라에서 영어 교육에 몸담고 있습니다. 감수한 책으로는《영어 필기체 10일 완성 노트》
《음악이 있는 팝송 영어 필사》가 있습니다.

개정보급판영어 필기체 100일 기적의 노트

1판 1쇄 발행 2022년 11월 15일
개정보급판 1쇄 발행 2024년 10월 25일
—
기획 · 구성 펜앤페이퍼(Pen&Paper) 감수 이지(Izzie)
—

펴낸이 김은중
편집 허선영 디자인 김순수
펴낸곳 가위바위보
출판 등록 2020년 11월 17일 제 2020-000316호
주소 경기도 부천시 소향로 25, 511호. (우편번호 14544)
팩스 02-6008-5011 전자우편 gbbbooks@naver.com
네이버블로그 gbbbooks 인스타그램 gbbbooks 페이스북 gbbbooks 트위터 gbb_books
—

ISBN 979-11-92156-30-9 13740

가위바위보 출판사는 나답게 만드는 책, 그리고 다함께 즐기는 책을 만듭니다.

100 Days of English Cursive Handwriting Miracle Workbook

개정보급판

영어 필기체 **100일** 기적의 노트

GBB

나의 글씨를 예술로 만들어주는
아름다운 영어 필기체!

최근 쓰기에 관심 가진 사람들이 크게 늘었어요. 뭔가를 쓰는 동안 사람들은 마음이 편안해지면서 여유를 가질 수 있고, 스스로를 돌아볼 수 있기 때문일 거예요.

그중에서도 특히 영어 필기체 쓰기는 많은 매력을 가지고 있어요.

첫 번째는 개성 표현이에요. 필기체는 자신만의 개성을 표현할 수 있는 좋은 방법이지요. 이 과정에서 자신감도 생겨요.

두 번째는 예술성이에요. 필기체는 그 자체로 예술적인 가치가 있어요. 아름다운 필기체는 보는 사람에게도 즐거움을 줄 수 있고, 카드나 편지 등을 쓸 때 더욱 특별한 느낌을 주지요. 아름다운 필기체를 연습하면, 하나의 예술 작품을 만드는 것과 같은 만족감을 줄 수 있어요.

세 번째는 두뇌 운동이에요. 연구에 따르면, 손으로 글을 쓰는 것은 타이핑보다 기억력 향상에 더 효과적이에요. 필기체를 따라 쓰면 뇌가 더 적극적으로 활동하게 되어 학습 효과가 높아지지요. 또 필기체를 따라 쓰는 과정은 꽤 많은 집중력이 필요해요. 필기체를 연습하면 자연스럽게 집중력도 향상되지요.

네 번째는 스트레스 해소예요. 필기체를 따라 쓰는 것은 일종의 명상과도 같아요. 규칙적인 패턴을 따라 글씨를 쓰는 과정에서 마음이 차분해지고 스트레스가 줄어들 수 있어요.

이처럼 필기체 쓰기는 단순히 글을 예쁘게 쓰는 것 이상의 많은 장점을 가지고 있어요. 꾸준히 연습을 통해 필기체를 익힌다면, 여러 방면에서 유용하게 활용할 수 있을 거예요.

✳ 다양한 그리드를 활용해 필기체 연습

영어 필기체를 아름답게 쓰려면 글자와 글자 사이의 간격과 높낮이, 각도를 고르게 하면서 조화롭게 어우러지도록 하는 것이 중요해요. 이를 위해서는 다양한 그리드에서 연습해 볼 필요가 있어요. 이 책에는 알파벳 필기체를 효율적으로 연습할 수 있도록 단계별 그리드를 수록했어요. 네 줄짜리 그리드 선에서 시작해 밑줄 그리드, 도트 그리드 등에서 다양하게 연습해 본 뒤, 마지막에는 아무것도 없는 빈 페이지에 자유롭게 써보세요. 체계적으로 영어 알파벳 필기체 연습을 할 수 있을 거예요.

✳ 아름다운 문장으로 즐거운 연습

단순히 영어 필기체를 예쁘게 쓰는 것도 중요하지만 문장의 내용을 즐기는 것도 의미 있어요. 이 책에는 세계 명작 속의 문장, 영화 속 명대사, 역사적인 연설문, 명언 등 다양한 자료에서 골라 뽑은 좋은 문장들이 가득하기 때문에 지루하지 않게 연습할 수 있어요. 영어 필기체로 문장을 쓰면서 소리내어 읽거나 외워보는 것도 영어 공부에 도움이 될 거예요.

✳ 짧은 문장에서 긴 문장까지, 단계별 연습

이 책은 한번에 쓸 수 있는 짧은 문장부터 점점 긴 문장으로 연습할 수 있도록 구성되어 있어요. 짧은 문장을 쓸 때는 각각의 알파벳의 모양을 정확하게 쓰고 끊기지 않도록 하는 데 집중하고, 긴 문장을 쓸 때는 전체적인 글자의 조화와 여백, 균형감을 생각하면서 쓰도록 노력해 보세요. 100일 동안 꾸준히 연습한다면 누구나 개성 넘치고 아름다운 자신만의 영어 필기체를 완성할 수 있을 거예요!

알파벳 대문자를 이어 써보세요.

ABCDEFGHIJKLMNOPQRSTUVWXYZ

ABCDEFGHIJKLMNOPQRSTUVWXYZ

ABCDEFGHIJKLMNOPQRSTUVWXYZ

알파벳 소문자를 한 번에 이어 써보세요. i, j, t, x의 점과 선은 마지막에 쓰세요.

abcdefghijklmnopqrstuvwxyz

abcdefghijklmnopqrstuvwxyz

abcdefghijklmnopqrstuvwxyz

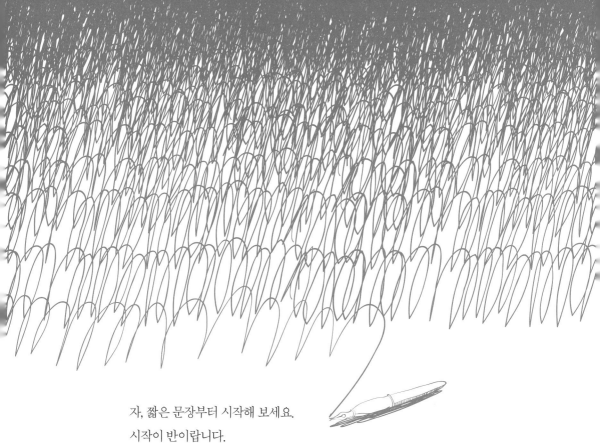

자, 짧은 문장부터 시작해 보세요.
시작이 반이랍니다.

Turn your wounds into wisdom.

Turn your wounds into wisdom.

Turn your wounds into wisdom.

Turn your wounds into wisdom.

상처를 지혜로 바꿔라. : 오프라 윈프리(방송인)

The most personal is the most creative.

The most personal is the most creative.

The most personal is the most creative.

The most personal is the most creative.

가장 개인적인 것이 가장 창의적인 것이다. : 마틴 스코세이지(영화감독)

The ocean is made of drops.

The ocean is made of drops.

The ocean is made of drops.

The ocean is made of drops.

바다는 작은 물방울로 만들어졌다. : 마더 테레사(수녀)

Wheresoever you go, go with all your heart.

Wheresoever you go, go with all your heart.

Wheresoever you go, go with all your heart.

Wheresoever you go, go with all your heart.

어디에 가든, 마음을 다하라. : 공자(철학자)

We will find a way. We always have.

We will find a way. We always have.

We will find a way. We always have.

We will find a way. We always have.

우리는 길을 찾을 것이다. 늘 그래왔듯이. : 영화 〈인터스텔라〉

A room without books is like a body without a soul.

A room without books is like a body without a soul.

A room without books is like a body without a soul.

A room without books is like a body without a soul.

책이 없는 방은 영혼이 없는 몸과 같다. : 키케로(로마 정치가)

You'll never find a rainbow if you are looking down.

You'll never find a rainbow if you are looking down.

You'll never find a rainbow if you are looking down.

You'll never find a rainbow if you are looking down.

고개를 숙이고 있으면 무지개를 찾을 수 없다. : 찰리 채플린(배우, 영화감독)

16

The secret of getting ahead is getting started.

The secret of getting ahead is getting started.

The secret of getting ahead is getting started.

The secret of getting ahead is getting started.

앞서가는 방법의 비밀은 시작하는 것이다. : 마크 트웨인(소설가)

Life is either a daring adventure or nothing at all.

Life is either a daring adventure or nothing at all.

Life is either a daring adventure or nothing at all.

Life is either a daring adventure or nothing at all.

인생은 대담한 모험이다. 그게 아니면 아무것도 아니다. : 헬렌 켈러(사회사업가)

I paint objects as I think them, not as I see them.

I paint objects as I think them, not as I see them.

I paint objects as I think them, not as I see them.

I paint objects as I think them, not as I see them.
나는 대상을 보는 대로가 아니라 생각한 대로 그린다. : 파블로 피카소(화가)

Education is the best provision for old age.

Education is the best provision for old age.

Education is the best provision for old age.

Education is the best provision for old age.

배움은 노년을 위한 가장 훌륭한 대책이다.

: 아리스토텔레스(고대 그리스 철학자)

Defining beauty is simply a matter of opinion.

Defining beauty is simply a matter of opinion.

Defining beauty is simply a matter of opinion.

Defining beauty is simply a matter of opinion.

아름다움의 정의는 단지 개인의 취향이다. : 데본 아오키(모델, 배우)

21

I felt that I breathed an atmosphere of sorrow.

I felt that I breathed an atmosphere of sorrow.

I felt that I breathed an atmosphere of sorrow.

I felt that I breathed an atmosphere of sorrow.

나는 슬픔의 공기를 마셨다고 느꼈다. : 에드거 앨런 포(시인)

If you're going through hell, keep going.

If you're going through hell, keep going.

If you're going through hell, keep going.

If you're going through hell, keep going.

만약 지옥을 겪고 있다면 계속 나아가라. : 윈스턴 처칠(영국 총리)

Love means never having to say you're sorry.

Love means never having to say you're sorry.

Love means never having to say you're sorry.

Love means never having to say you're sorry.
사랑이란 미안하다는 말을 할 필요가 없게 행동하는 것이다.
: 영화 〈러브 스토리〉

Everyone deserves not just to survive, but to live.

Everyone deserves not just to survive, but to live.

Everyone deserves not just to survive, but to live.

Everyone deserves not just to survive, but to live.

모든 사람은 단지 생존할 자격이 있는 게 아니라 살 자격이 있는 것이다.

: 스티브 매퀸(영화감독)

Life is what happens

while you are busy making other plans.

Life is what happens

while you are busy making other plans.

Life is what happens

while you are busy making other plans.

Life is what happens
while you are busy making other plans.

인생이란 다른 계획을 세우는 동안 일어나는 것이다.
: 존 레논(가수, 비틀즈)

What would life be

if we had no courage to attempt anything?

What would life be

if we had no courage to attempt anything?

What would life be

if we had no courage to attempt anything?

What would life be
if we had no courage to attempt anything?

우리에게 무언가 시도할 용기가 없다면 삶은 어떻게 될까?
: 빈센트 반 고흐(화가)

I am grateful for what I am and have.

My thanksgiving is perpetual.

I am grateful for what I am and have.

My thanksgiving is perpetual.

I am grateful for what I am and have.

My thanksgiving is perpetual.

I am grateful for what I am and have.
My thanksgiving is perpetual.

지금의 내 모습과 지금 내가 가진 것에 감사한다.
나의 감사는 끊임없이 계속된다. : 헨리 데이비드 소로(작가)

28

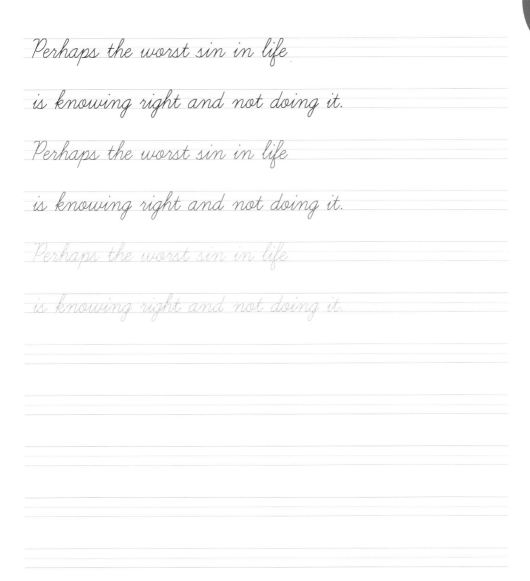

Perhaps the worst sin in life
is knowing right and not doing it.

Perhaps the worst sin in life
is knowing right and not doing it.

Perhaps the worst sin in life
is knowing right and not doing it.

Perhaps the worst sin in life
is knowing right and not doing it.

아마도 살면서 가장 최악의 죄는 옳은 것을 알면서도 실천하지 않는 것이다.
: 마틴 루터 킹(목사, 인권운동가)

Life isn't about finding yourself.

Life is about creating yourself.

Life isn't about finding yourself.

Life is about creating yourself.

Life isn't about finding yourself.

Life is about creating yourself.

Life isn't about finding yourself.
Life is about creating yourself.

인생은 너 자신을 찾는 것이 아니다. 너 자신을 창조하는 것이다.
: 조지 버나드 쇼(작가)

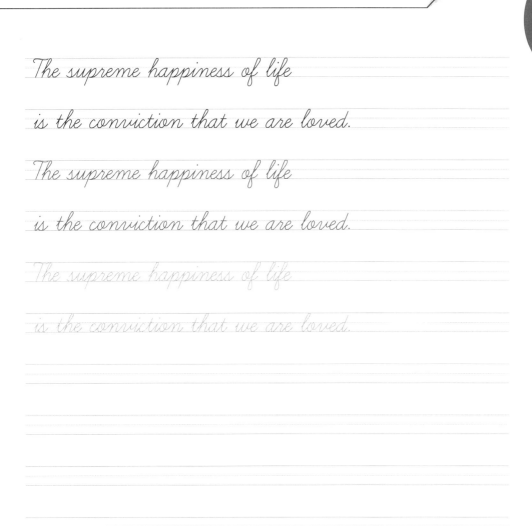

The supreme happiness of life
is the conviction that we are loved.
The supreme happiness of life
is the conviction that we are loved.
The supreme happiness of life
is the conviction that we are loved.

The supreme happiness of life
is the conviction that we are loved.

삶의 최고의 행복은 우리가 사랑받고 있다는 확신이다.

: 빅토르 위고(작가)

Nature never deceives us;

it is always we who deceive ourselves.

Nature never deceives us;

it is always we who deceive ourselves.

Nature never deceives us;

it is always we who deceive ourselves.

Nature never deceives us;
it is always we who deceive ourselves.

자연은 인간을 결코 속이지 않는다.
우리를 속이는 것은 항상 우리 자신이다. : 장 자크 루소(사상가, 작가)

Man is not made for defeat.

A man can be destroyed but not defeated.

Man is not made for defeat.

A man can be destroyed but not defeated.

Man is not made for defeat.

A man can be destroyed but not defeated.

Man is not made for defeat.
A man can be destroyed but not defeated.

인간은 패배하도록 만들어지지 않았다.
파괴될 수는 있어도 절대 패배할 수 없다. : 어니스트 헤밍웨이 《노인과 바다》

33

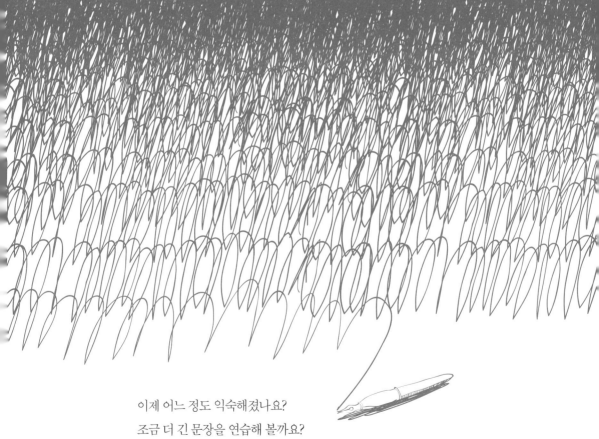

이제 어느 정도 익숙해졌나요?
조금 더 긴 문장을 연습해 볼까요?

Happy families are all alike;
every unhappy family is unhappy in its own way.

Happy families are all alike;
every unhappy family is unhappy in its own way.

행복한 가족은 모두 비슷비슷하지만,
불행한 가족은 저마다의 이유로 불행하다. : 레프 톨스토이 《안나 카레니나》

It was a bright cold day in April,
and the clocks were striking thirteen.

It was a bright cold day in April,
and the clocks were striking thirteen.

4월의 맑고 쌀쌀한 어느 날, 시계가 13시를 가리켰다.
: 조지 오웰 《1984》

Life is like a box of chocolates,
you never know what you're gonna get.

Life is like a box of chocolates,
you never know what you're gonna get.

인생은 마치 초콜릿 상자와도 같아서,
무엇을 얻게 될지 모른다. : 영화 〈포레스트 검프〉

If I had eight hours to chop down a tree,
I'd spend six hours sharpening my ax.

If I had eight hours to chop down a tree,
I'd spend six hours sharpening my ax.

나무를 자를 8시간이 있다면 나는 도끼를 가는 데
6시간을 쓸 것이다. : 에이브러햄 링컨(미국 대통령)

39

If I have seen further,
it is by standing on the shoulders of Giants.

If I have seen further,
it is by standing on the shoulders of Giants.

내가 더 멀리 볼 수 있었다면,
그것은 거인들의 어깨 위에 서 있었기 때문이다. : 아이작 뉴턴(물리학자)

Tomorrow I'll think of some way to get him back. After all, tomorrow is another day.

Tomorrow I'll think of some way to get him back.
After all, tomorrow is another day.

내일 그를 되찾을 방법을 생각해 봐야지.
어쨌든, 내일은 내일의 태양이 뜰 테니까. : 영화 〈바람과 함께 사라지다〉

It is a narrow mind which cannot look at
a subject from various points of view.

It is a narrow mind which cannot look at
a subject from various points of view.

편협한 마음은 주제를 다양한 관점에서 바라볼 수 없다.

: 조지 엘리엇 《미들마치》

All we can know is that we know nothing.
And that's the height of human wisdom.

All we can know is that we know nothing.
And that's the height of human wisdom.

우리가 알 수 있는 것은 우리가 아무것도 모른다는 것뿐이다.
그것이 인간 지혜의 절정이다. : 레프 톨스토이 《전쟁과 평화》

43

I can shake off everything as I write;
my sorrows disappear, my courage is reborn.

I can shake off everything as I write;
my sorrows disappear, my courage is reborn.

나는 글을 쓸 때 모든 것을 떨쳐버릴 수 있다.
나의 슬픔은 사라지고, 나의 용기는 다시 태어난다.

: 안네 프랑크《안네의 일기》저자)

Live as if you were to die tomorrow.

Learn as if you were to live forever.

Live as if you were to die tomorrow.
Learn as if you were to live forever.

내일 죽을 것처럼 살라. 영원히 살 것처럼 배우라.

: 마하트마 간디(정치지도자)

If life were predictable, it would cease to be life, and be without flavor.

If life were predictable, it would cease to be life, and be without flavor.

삶이 예측 가능하다면 생명력도, 향기도 없을 것이다.

: 엘리너 루스벨트(인권운동가)

It is not how much we have,
but how much we enjoy, that makes happiness.

It is not how much we have,
but how much we enjoy, that makes happiness.

행복은 가진 것이 얼마나 많은지가 아니라,
인생을 얼마나 즐기는지에 달려 있다. : 찰스 스펄전(성직자)

The great glory in living, lies not in never falling but rising every time we fall.

The great glory in living, lies not
in never falling but rising every time we fall.

인생의 가장 큰 영광은 절대 쓰러지지 않는 것이 아니라,
쓰러질 때마다 일어나는 것이다. : 넬슨 만델라(남아공 대통령)

There is no man living who isn't capable of doing more than he thinks he can do.

There is no man living who isn't capable
of doing more than he thinks he can do.

사람은 누구나 자기가 할 수 있다고 믿는 것 이상의 것을 할 수 있다.
: 헨리 포드(기업인)

It is only with the heart that one can see rightly; what is essential is invisible to the eye.

It is only with the heart that one can see rightly;
what is essential is invisible to the eye.

마음으로만 제대로 볼 수 있다. 본질적인 것은 눈에 보이지 않는다.
: 앙투안 드 생텍쥐페리 〈어린 왕자〉

Waste no more time talking about great souls and how they should be, become one yourself.

Waste no more time talking about great souls and how they should be, become one yourself.

위인이나 위인의 조건에 대한 논쟁으로 시간을 낭비하지 말고,
너 자신이 위인이 **되라.** : 마르쿠스 아우렐리우스(로마 황제)

54

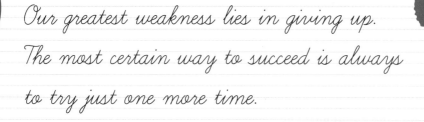

Our greatest weakness lies in giving up.
The most certain way to succeed is always
to try just one more time.

Our greatest weakness lies in giving up.
The most certain way to succeed is always
to try just one more time.

우리의 가장 큰 약점은 포기하는 데 있다.
성공으로 가는 가장 확실한 방법은 언제든지 한 번 더 시도해 보는 것이다.
: 토머스 에디슨(발명가)

I have learned to seek my happiness by limiting my desires, rather than in attempting to satisfy them.

I have learned to seek my happiness
by limiting my desires, rather than
in attempting to satisfy them.

나는 욕망을 만족시키려고 하기보다는 제한함으로써
행복을 찾는 법을 배웠다. : 존 스튜어트 밀(경제학자)

DAY 43

Our anxiety does not come from
thinking about the future,
but from wanting to control it.

Our anxiety does not come from
thinking about the future,
but from wanting to control it.

우리의 불안은 미래의 걱정에서 오는 것이 아니라
그것을 통제하고 싶은 데서 비롯된다. : 칼릴 지브란(작가)

I like nonsense, it wakes up the brain cells.

Fantasy is a necessary ingredient in living.

I like nonsense, it wakes up the brain cells.
Fantasy is a necessary ingredient in living.

나는 비상식적인 걸 좋아한다. 그것은 뇌를 깨우기 때문이다.
환상은 삶을 살아가는 데 꼭 필요하다. : 닥터 수스(동화작가)

The good is defined by us, it is practiced,
it is invented. And this is a collective work.

The good is defined by us, it is practiced,
it is invented. And this is a collective work.

선은 우리에 의해 정의되고, 실행되고, 발명된다.
그리고 그것은 함께하는 작업이다. : 미셸 푸코(철학자)

For sweetest things turn sourest by their deeds;
Lillies that fester smell far worse than weeds.

For sweetest things turn sourest by their deeds;
Lillies that fester smell far worse than weeds.

가장 달콤한 것이 가장 심하게 부패한다.
썩어가는 백합은 잡초보다 훨씬 더 악취가 난다. : 윌리엄 셰익스피어 《소네트》

The sad thruth is that most evil is done by people who never make up their minds to be good or evil.

The sad thruth is that most evil is done by people who never make up their minds to be good or evil.

슬픈 진실은 대부분의 악이 선하려고 하거나 악하려고
마음먹지 않은 사람들에 의해 행해진다는 것이다. : 해나 아렌트(철학자)

If you are not willing to learn, no one can help you.

If you are determined to learn, no one can stop you.

If you are not willing to learn, no one can help you.
If you are determined to learn, no one can stop you.

당신이 배우려고 하지 않는다면, 아무도 당신을 도와줄 수 없다.
당신이 배우겠다고 마음먹으면, 아무도 당신을 막을 수 없다.
: 지그 지글러(작가, 연설가)

DAY 49

Develop success from failures.
Discouragement and failures are two of the surest
stepping stones to success.

Develop success from failures.
Discouragement and failures are two of the surest
stepping stones to success.

실패로부터 성공을 발전시켜라.
낙담과 실패는 성공으로 가는 가장 확실한 두 가지 디딤돌이다.
: 데일 카네기(작가)

If he loved with all the powers of his puny being,
he couldn't love as much in eighty years as
I could in a day.

If he loved with all the powers of his puny being,
he couldn't love as much in eighty years as
I could in a day.

만약 그가 그의 하찮은 존재의 모든 힘을 다해 사랑했다면,
그는 내가 하루에 할 수 있는 것처럼 80년 동안 사랑할 수 없었을 것이다.
: 에밀리 브론테 《폭풍의 언덕》

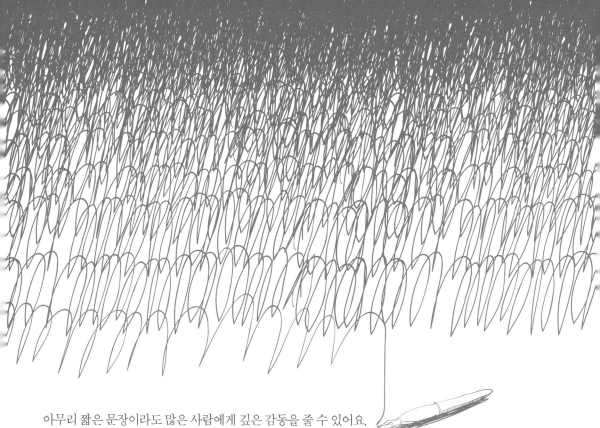

아무리 짧은 문장이라도 많은 사람에게 깊은 감동을 줄 수 있어요.
당신의 필기체로 감동의 문장을 써보세요.

From a child I was fond of reading,
and all the little money that came into
my hands was ever laid out in books.

From a child I was fond of reading,
and all the little money that came into
my hands was ever laid out in books.

어린 시절부터 나는 독서를 좋아했고,
내 손에 쥐어지는 모든 푼돈은 책을 위해 썼다. : 벤저민 프랭클린〈자서전〉

It is a truth universally acknowledged,
that a single man in possession of a good fortune,
must be in want of a wife.

It is a truth universally acknowledged,
that a single man in possession of a good fortune,
must be in want of a wife.

재산이 많은 독신 남자에게 아내가 필요하다고 확신하는 것은
보편적으로 인정되는 사실이다. : 제인 오스틴 〈오만과 편견〉

Nothing in life is to be feared, it is only to be understood. Now is the time to understand more, so that we may fear less.

Nothing in life is to be feared, it is only to be
understood. Now is the time to understand more,
so that we may fear less.

인생의 어떤 것도 두려워할 필요가 없다.
그것은 단지 이해되어야 할 문제일 뿐이다.
두려워하지 않도록 지금 우리는 더 많이 이해해야 한다. : 마리 퀴리(물리화학자)

I am no bird; and no net ensnares me;
I am a free human being, with an independent will;
which I now exert to leave you.

I am no bird; and no net ensnares me;
I am a free human being, with an independent will;
which I now exert to leave you.

나는 새가 아니다. 어떤 그물도 나를 옭아매지 못한다.
나는 독립적인 의지를 가진 자유로운 인간이며,
이제 당신을 떠나기 위해 노력하고자 한다. : 샬롯 브론테 《제인 에어》

The difference between successful people and really successful people is that really successful people say no to almost everything.

The difference between successful people
and really successful people is that really
successful people say no to almost everything.

성공적인 사람들과 뛰어나게 성공적인 사람들의 차이라면,
정말 성공적인 사람들은 거의 모든 것에 아니오를 말한다는 점이다.

: 워렌 버핏(기업가)

Fantasy love is much better than reality love.
Never doing it is very exciting.
The most exciting attractions are between
two opposites that never meet.

Fantasy love is much better than reality love.
Never doing it is very exciting.
The most exciting attractions are between
two opposites that never meet.

현실 속 사랑보다 환상 속 사랑이 훨씬 낫다.
절대로 사랑하지 않는 것은 매우 흥미롭다.
가장 흥미진진한 매력은 결코 만나지 않은 두 개의 상반됨 사이에 있다.
: 앤디 워홀(미술가, 영화제작자)

The most successful people in life recognize
that in life they create their own love,
they manufacture their own meaning,
they generate their own motivation.

The most successful people in life recognize
that in life they create their own love,
they manufacture their own meaning,
they generate their own motivation.

가장 성공한 사람들은 인생에서 자신만의 사랑을 만들고, 의미를 만든다.
자신만의 원동력을 만든다는 것을 인식한다. : 닐 타이슨(천체물리학자)

You can't stay in your corner of the Forest
waiting for others to come to you.
You have to go to them sometimes.

You can't stay in your corner of the Forest
waiting for others to come to you.
You have to go to them sometimes.

다른 이들이 너에게 올 때까지 숲속 구석에 머무를 순 없어.
가끔은 네가 그들에게 다가가야 해. _앨런 알렉산더 밀른 〈곰돌이 푸〉_

Most of the important things in the world have been accomplished by people who have kept on trying when there seemed to be no hope at all.

Most of the important things in the world
have been accomplished by people who have kept
on trying when there seemed to be no hope at all.

세상에서 중요한 것 중 대부분은 희망이 보이지 않는 상황에서도
끊임없이 도전한 사람들이 이룬 것이다. : 데일 카네기 《인간관계론》

94

To me, it underscores our responsibility to deal more kindly with one another, and to preserve and cherish the pale blue dot, the only home we've ever known.

To me, it underscores our responsibility to deal more kindly with one another, and to preserve and cherish the pale blue dot, the only home we've ever known.

나에게 이 사진은, 우리가 서로를 더 배려해야 하고 우리가 아는 유일한 삶의 터전인 저 희미한 푸른 점을 아끼고 보존해야 한다는 책임감을 강조한다. : 칼 세이건(천문학자)

My motivation is love for life, love for my kids and people I know and don't know and love for our planet and the Universe. It never stops.

My motivation is love for life, love for my kids
and people I know and don't know and love for
our planet and the Universe. It never stops.

내 원동력은 삶에 대한 사랑,
내 아이들과 내가 알거나 모르는 사람들에 대한 사랑,
지구와 우주에 대한 사랑이다. 이것은 절대 멈추지 않는다. : 오노 요코(가수)

It is high time that humanity went beyond Earth.
Should have a moon base by now and sent
astronauts to Mars. The future needs to inspire.

It is high time that humanity went beyond Earth.
Should have a moon base by now and sent
astronauts to Mars. The future needs to inspire.

인류가 지구를 넘어설 때가 되었다. 지금쯤 달 기지가 있어야 하고
화성에 우주비행사를 보냈어야 했다. 미래는 영감을 주는 것을 필요로 한다.
: 일론 머스크(기업가)

It is impossible to live without failing at something,
unless you live so cautiously
that you might as well not have lived at all;
in which case, you fail by default.

It is impossible to live without failing
at something, unless you live so cautiously
that you might as well not have lived at all;
in which case, you fail by default.

실패하지 않고 사는 것은 불가능하다.
그렇게 조심스럽게 산다면, 전혀 살지 않은 것과 마찬가지다.
이 경우 기본적으로 실패한다. : 조앤 롤링(작가)

Change will not come if we wait for some
other person, or if we wait for some other time.
We are the ones we've been waiting for.
We are the change that we seek.

Change will not come if we wait for some
other person, or if we wait for some other time.
We are the ones we've been waiting for.
We are the change that we seek.

다른 사람이 가져오는 변화나 더 좋은 시기를 기다리기만 한다면
결국 변화는 오지 않을 것이다. 우리 자신이 바로 우리가 기다리던 사람들이다.
우리 자신이 바로 우리가 찾는 변화다. 바락 오바마(미국 대통령)

We played robber now and then about a month,
and then I resigned. All the boys did.
We hadn't robbed nobody, hadn't killed any people,
but only just pretended.

We played robber now and then about a month,
and then I resigned. All the boys did.
We hadn't robbed nobody, hadn't killed any people,
but only just pretended.

우리는 강도 놀이를 하다가 한 달쯤 후엔 그만두었다.
모든 소년들이 그랬다. 우리는 아무도 강탈하지 않았고,
사람을 죽이지도 않았고, 그저 시늉만 했다. 마크 트웨인 《허클베리 핀의 모험》

The creatures outside looked from pig to man,
and from man to pig, and from pig to man again;
but already it was impossible to say
which was which.

The creatures outside looked from pig to man,
and from man to pig, and from pig to man again;
but already it was impossible to say which was which.

창밖의 동물들은 돼지로부터 사람에게, 사람으로부터 돼지에게,
다시 돼지로부터 사람에게 번갈아 시선을 옮겼다.
그러나 이미 누가 돼지고 누가 사람인지 분간하기는 어려웠다.
: 조지 오웰 《동물 농장》

Nello rose to his feet and stretched his arms to them;
the tears of a passionate ecstasy glistened on the
paleness of his face. "I have seen them at last!"
he cried aloud. "O God, it is enough!"

Nello rose to his feet and stretched his arms to them;
the tears of a passionate ecstasy glistened on the
paleness of his face. "I have seen them at last!"
he cried aloud. "O God, it is enough!"

네로는 일어서서 그림 쪽으로 팔을 뻗었다. 창백한 얼굴에 환희의 눈물이 흘렀다.
"드디어 봤어요!" 그는 큰 소리로 외쳤다.
"오, 신이시여, 그것으로 충분합니다!" : 위다 《플랜더스의 개》

Friendship is the hardest thing in the world
to explain. It's not something you learn in school.
But if you haven't learned the meaning of friendship,
you really haven't learned anything.

Friendship is the hardest thing in the world
to explain. It's not something you learn in school.
But if you haven't learned the meaning of friendship,
you really haven't learned anything.

우정은 세상에서 가장 설명하기 어려운 것이며,
학교에서 배우는 것도 아니다. 하지만 우정의 의미를 배우지 않았다면
당신은 정말 아무것도 배우지 못한 것이다. : 무하마드 알리(권투선수)

The tiger's roar filled the cave with thunder.
Mother Wolf shook herself clear of the cubs
and sprang forward, her eyes, like two green moons
in the darkness, facing the blazing eyes
of Shere Khan.

The tiger's roar filled the cave with thunder.
Mother Wolf shook herself clear of the cubs
and sprang forward, her eyes, like two green moons
in the darkness, facing the blazing eyes of Shere Khan.

천둥 같은 호랑이의 포효가 동굴을 가득 채웠다. 어미 늑대는 새끼들에게서
떨어져 앞으로 뛰쳐나갔고, 어둠 속에 빛나는 두 개의 초록색 달과
같은 눈으로 셰어칸의 이글거리는 눈을 노려보았다. : 러디어드 키플링 《정글 북》

The clock indicated a quarter before nine
when he appeared in the great saloon.
Phileas Fogg had accomplished the journey round
the world in eighty days! Phileas Fogg had won
his wager of twenty thousand pounds!

The clock indicated a quarter before nine
when he appeared in the great saloon.
Phileas Fogg had accomplished the journey round
the world in eighty days! Phileas Fogg had won
his wager of twenty thousand pounds!

시계가 8시 45분을 가리켰을 때, 그가 큰 휴게실에 나타났다.
필리어스 포그는 80일 만에 세계 일주를 해낸 것이다!
그는 내기에 걸었던 2만 파운드를 땄다. · 쥘 베른 《80일간의 세계일주》

Instead of learning from other people's success, learn from their mistakes. Most of the people who fail share common reason whereas success can be attributed to various different kinds of reasons.

Instead of learning from other people's success,
learn from their mistakes. Most of the people
who fail share common reason whereas success
can be attributed to various different kinds of reasons.

다른 사람의 성공보다 실패에서 배움을 얻어라.
실패하는 대부분의 사람에게는 공통된 이유가 있게 마련이지만,
성공은 여러 요인이 작용하는 결과물일 수 있다. :미원(기업가)

I believe the nicest and sweetest days are not those
on which anything very splendid or wonderful
or exciting happens but just those that bring simple
little pleasures, following one another softly,
like pearls slipping off a string.

I believe the nicest and sweetest days are not those
on which anything very splendid or wonderful
or exciting happens but just those that bring simple
little pleasures, following one another softly,
like pearls slipping off a string.

정말로 즐겁고 행복한 나날이란 멋지고 놀라운 일이 일어나는 날이 아니에요.
진주 알들이 알알이 한 줄로 꿰어지듯이, 소박하고 작은 기쁨들이
조용히 이어지는 날들이에요. : 루시 모드 몽고메리 《빨강머리 앤》

The Count halted, putting down my bags,
closed the door, and crossing the room,
opened another door, which led into a small
octagonal room lit by a single lamp,
and seemingly without a window of any sort.

The Count halted, putting down my bags,
closed the door, and crossing the room,
opened another door, which led into a small
octagonal room lit by a single lamp,
and seemingly without a window of any sort.

백작은 걸음을 멈추고, 내 가방들을 내려놓고는 문을 닫았다.
그리고 방을 가로질러 또 다른 문을 열었다. 그 방은 램프 하나가 켜져 있는
작은 팔각형 모양이었는데, 창문은 없는 것 같았다. :브램 스토커 〈드라큘라〉

I stuffed a shirt or two into my old carpet-bag,
tucked it under my arm, and started for Cape Horn
and the Pacific. Quitting the good city of old Manhatto,
I duly arrived in New Bedford.
It was a Saturday night in December.

I stuffed a shirt or two into my old carpet-bag,
tucked it under my arm, and started for Cape Horn
and the Pacific. Quitting the good city of old Manhatto,
I duly arrived in New Bedford.
It was a Saturday night in December.

나는 낡은 여행용 가방에 셔츠 한두 장을 챙겨 넣고는
케이프 혼과 태평양으로 출발했다. 멋진 도시인 맨해튼을 떠나
뉴베드퍼드에 도착했다. 12월의 토요일 밤이었다. : 허먼 멜빌 《모비딕》

124

The poor little Swallow grew colder and colder,
but he would not leave the Prince, he loved him
too well. He picked up crumbs outside the baker's door
when the baker was not looking and tried
to keep himself warm by flapping his wings.

The poor little Swallow grew colder and colder,
but he would not leave the Prince, he loved him
too well. He picked up crumbs outside
the baker's door when the baker was not looking
and tried to keep himself warm by flapping his wings.

점점 더 추워졌지만 가엾은 제비는 왕자를 너무 사랑했기에 그의 곁을
떠나지 않았다. 제비는 주인이 보고 있지 않으면 빵집 문 앞에서 빵 부스러기를
쪼아 먹었고, 날갯짓을 하며 몸을 따뜻하게 만들려고 했다.
: 오스카 와일드 《행복한 왕자》

126

필기체가 어느 정도 손에 익었나요?
이제 문학 작품 등 긴 문장을 써보면서
나만의 손글씨를 만들어 가세요.

I don't believe in competition.
How can I win over Glenn Close?
I've been watching her so many performances.
All the nominees, five nominees,
we are the winner for the different movie.
We played the different role,
so we cannot compete each other.

I don't believe in competition.
How can I win over Glenn Close?
I've been watching her so many performances.
All the nominees, five nominees,
we are the winner for the different movie.
We played the different role,
so we cannot compete each other.

나는 경쟁을 믿지 않습니다. 내가 어떻게 글렌 클로즈를 이길 수 있나요?
나는 그녀의 훌륭한 연기를 많이 봐왔습니다. 다섯 명의 후보들은
모두 각기 다른 영화의 수상자입니다. 우리는 모두 다른 역할을 했고,
그렇기에 우리는 서로 경쟁할 수가 없습니다. : 윤여정(배우)

Then the Spring came, and all over the country there were little blossoms and little birds. Only in the garden of the Selfish Giant it was still winter. The birds did not care to sing in it as there were no children, and the trees forgot to blossom.

Then the Spring came, and all over the country there were little blossoms and little birds. Only in the garden of the Selfish Giant it was still winter. The birds did not care to sing in it as there were no children, and the trees forgot to blossom.

봄이 되자 온 나라에 작은 꽃이 피었고 작은 새들이 날아왔다.
이기적인 거인의 정원만 아직도 겨울이었다. 새들은 아이들이 없는
그곳에서 노래하려고 하지 않았고, 나무들도 싹 틔우는 것을 잊어버렸다.
: 오스카 와일드 《거인의 정원》

"Would you tell me, please,
which way I ought to go from here?"
"That depends a good deal on
where you want to get to," said the Cat.
"I don't much care where —" said Alice.
"Then it doesn't matter which way you go,"
said the Cat.

"Would you tell me, please,
which way I ought to go from here?"
"That depends a good deal on
where you want to get to," said the Cat.
"I don't much care where—" said Alice.
"Then it doesn't matter which way you go,"
said the Cat.

"여기서 어디로 가야 하는지 알려주시겠어요?"
"그건 어디로 가고 싶은지에 달렸지." 체셔 고양이가 말했다.
"어디든 상관없어—." 앨리스가 말했다.
"그럼 어느 쪽으로 가도 상관없겠네." 체셔 고양이가 말했다.
: 루이스 캐럴 〈이상한 나라의 앨리스〉

The important thing is not to stop questioning.
Curiosity has its own reason for existing.
One cannot help but be in awe when he contemplates
the mysteries of eternity, of life, of the marvelous
structure of reality. It is enough if one tries merely
to comprehend a little of this mystery every day.
Never lose a holy curiosity.

The important thing is not to stop questioning.
Curiosity has its own reason for existing.
One cannot help but be in awe when he contemplates
the mysteries of eternity, of life, of the marvelous
structure of reality. It is enough if one tries merely
to comprehend a little of this mystery every day.
Never lose a holy curiosity.

가장 중요한 것은 질문을 멈추지 않는 것이다. 호기심은 그 자체만으로도
존재 이유를 갖는다. 영원, 삶 그리고 현실의 놀라움 구조에 대한 신비함을
생각해 볼 때 우리는 경외심을 느낄 수밖에 없다.
매일 이러한 신비함을 조금씩 이해하려고 노력하는 것만으로도 충분하다.
신성한 호기심을 절대로 잃지 마라. : 알베르트 아인슈타인(과학자)

She went through the door and found that it was a garden with walls all round it and that it was only one of several walled gardens which seemed to open into one another. She saw another open green door, revealing bushes and pathways between beds containing winter vegetables.

She went through the door and found that it was a garden with walls all round it and that it was only one of several walled gardens which seemed to open into one another. She saw another open green door, revealing bushes and pathways between beds containing winter vegetables.

그녀는 문으로 들어가서 사방이 담으로 둘러싸인 정원을 발견했다. 그곳은 담에 있는 문을 통해 서로 이어져 있는 것처럼 보이는 여러 정원 중의 하나였다. 그녀는 또 다른 초록색 문을 보았는데, 열려 있는 문으로 겨울 채소가 심어진 화단 사이에 있는 오솔길과 덤불이 보였다.

: 프랜시스 호지슨 버넷 《비밀의 정원》

One of the lessons that I grew up with was to always stay true to yourself and never let what somebody else says distract you from your goals.
And so when I hear about negative and false attacks, I really don't invest any energy in them, because I know who I am.

One of the lessons that I grew up with was to always
stay true to yourself and never let what somebody
else says distract you from your goals.
And so when I hear about negative and false attacks,
I really don't invest any energy in them,
because I know who I am.

내가 자라면서 얻은 교훈 중 하나는 항상 내 자신에게 솔직하고
절대 다른 사람이 말하는 것이 내 목표로부터 나를 방해하지 않게 하는 것이다.
그래서 부정적인 공격과 거짓 공격을 받아도
나는 내가 누구인지 알기 때문에 그것에 에너지를 쓰지 않는다.
: 미셸 오바마(미국 오바마 대통령 부인)

The cabin of Uncle Tom was a small log building,
close adjoining to "the house," as the negro
par excellence designates his master's dwelling.
In front it had a neat garden-patch, where,
every summer, strawberries, raspberries,
and a variety of fruits and vegetables,
flourished under careful tending.

The cabin of Uncle Tom was a small log building,
close adjoining to "the house," as the negro
par excellence designates his master's dwelling.
In front it had a neat garden-patch, where,
every summer, strawberries, raspberries,
and a variety of fruits and vegetables,
flourished under careful tending.

톰 아저씨의 오두막은 작은 통나무집이었고, 그 뛰어난 흑인이
주인집을 부르는 '저택' 가까이에 있었다. 그 앞에는 잘 정돈된
텃밭이 있었는데, 매년 여름마다 딸기, 산딸기,
다양한 과일과 채소가 세심한 보살핌 덕분에 잘 자랐다.
: 해리엇 비처 스토 《톰 아저씨의 오두막》

Your work is going to fill a large part of your life, and the only way to be truly satisfied is to do what you believe is great work. And the only way to do great work is to love what you do. If you haven't found it yet, keep looking. Don't settle. As with all matters of the heart, you'll know when you find it.

Your work is going to fill a large part of your life, and the only way to be truly satisfied is to do what you believe is great work. And the only way to do great work is to love what you do. If you haven't found it yet, keep looking. Don't settle. As with all matters of the heart, you'll know when you find it.

여러분의 일은 인생에서 큰 부분을 차지하게 될 것이고,
진정 만족하는 일을 하는 유일한 방법은 당신이 하는 일이 훌륭한 일이라고
믿는 것이다. 그리고 그 훌륭한 일을 하는 유일한 방법은 당신이 하는 일을
사랑하는 것이다. 만약 아직 찾지 못했다면 계속 찾아라. 안주하지 마라.
모든 일이 그렇듯이 그 일을 발견할 때 당신은 알 것이다. : 스티브 잡스(기업가)

When Scrooge awoke, it was so dark,
that looking out of bed, he could scarcely distinguish
the transparent window from the opaque walls of
his chamber. He was endeavouring to pierce
the darkness with his ferret eyes, when the chimes
of a neighbouring church struck the four quarters.
So he listened for the hour.

When Scrooge awoke, it was so dark,
that looking out of bed, he could scarcely distinguish
the transparent window from the opaque walls of
his chamber. He was endeavouring to pierce
the darkness with his ferret eyes, when the chimes
of a neighbouring church struck the four quarters.
So he listened for the hour.

스크루지가 잠에서 깨어났을 때, 너무 어두워서 투명한 창문과 방의
불투명한 벽을 구별할 수 없었다. 그는 흰 족제비와 같은 눈으로
어둠을 뚫어지게 쳐다보았다. 이웃 교회의 종소리가 사방에 울렸다.
그는 한 시간 동안 귀를 기울였다. : 찰스 디킨스 《크리스마스 캐럴》

We must fight against the spirit of
unconscious cruelty with which we treat the animals.
Animals suffer as much as we do.
True humanity does not allow us to impose such
sufferings on them.
It is our duty to make the whole world recognize it.
Until we extend our circle of compassion
to all living things, humanity will not find peace.

We must fight against the spirit of
unconscious cruelty with which we treat the animals.
Animals suffer as much as we do.
True humanity does not allow us to impose such
sufferings on them.
It is our duty to make the whole world recognize it.
Until we extend our circle of compassion
to all living things, humanity will not find peace.

우리는 우리가 동물을 대하는 무의식적인 잔인함에 맞서 싸워야 한다.
동물도 우리만큼 고통을 받는다.
진정한 인간성은 우리가 동물들에게 그러한 고통을 주는 것을
허락하지 않는 것이다. 전 세계 사람들에게 그것을 깨닫게 하는 것이
우리의 의무이다. 모든 생명체에게 연민의 범위를 넓혀나갈 때까지
인류는 평화를 찾지 못할 것이다. : 알베르트 슈바이처(의사)

"You see," he continued confidentially, "I don't mind my legs and arms and body being stuffed, because I cannot get hurt. If anyone treads on my toes or sticks a pin into me, it doesn't matter, for I can't feel it. But I do not want people to call me a fool, and if my head stays stuffed with straw instead of with brains, as yours is, how am I ever to know anything?"

"You see," he continued confidentially, "I don't mind my legs and arms and body being stuffed, because I cannot get hurt. If anyone treads on my toes or sticks a pin into me, it doesn't matter, for I can't feel it. But I do not want people to call me a fool, and if my head stays stuffed with straw instead of with brains, as yours is, how am I ever to know anything?"

"너도 알다시피, 나는 다칠 염려가 없으니까 다리와 팔과 몸이 지푸라기로 채워져도 상관없어. 나는 느끼지 못하니까 누가 내 발가락을 밟거나 핀으로 찔러도 괜찮아. 그러나 나는 사람들이 날 바보라고 부르는 것은 원하지 않아. 내 머리가 너처럼 뇌가 아니라 지푸라기로 채워져 있다면 평생 내가 어떻게 아는 것이 있을 수 있겠어?" : 프랭크 바움 《오즈의 마법사》

All of us had an ample share of the treasure and used it wisely or foolishly, according to our natures. Captain Smollett is now retired from the sea. Gray not only saved his money, but being suddenly smit with the desire to rise, also studied his profession, and he is now mate and part owner of a fine full-rigged ship, married besides, and the father of a family.

All of us had an ample share of the treasure
and used it wisely or foolishly, according to our natures.
Captain Smollett is now retired from the sea.
Gray not only saved his money, but being suddenly
smit with the desire to rise, also studied
his profession, and he is now mate and part owner
of a fine full-rigged ship, married besides,
and the father of a family.

우리는 모두 보물을 충분히 나누어 가졌고,
그것을 각자의 천성에 따라 현명하게도, 어리석게도 사용했다.
스몰렛 선장은 바다에서 은퇴했다. 그레이는 돈을 모으기도 했고,
갑자기 성공하고픈 욕망에 사로잡혀 직업을 얻기 위해 공부도 했다.
이제 그는 항해사이자 장비를 잘 갖춘 배의 공동 소유자가 되었으며
결혼도 하고 한 가정의 아버지가 되었다. : 로버트 루이스 스티븐슨 〈보물섬〉

Tom appeared on the sidewalk with a bucket of
whitewash and a long-handled brush.
He surveyed the fence, and all gladness left him
and a deep melancholy settled down upon his spirit.
Thirty yards of board fence nine feet high.
Life to him seemed hollow, and existence but a burden.

Tom appeared on the sidewalk with a bucket of
whitewash and a long-handled brush.
He surveyed the fence, and all gladness left him
and a deep melancholy settled down upon his spirit.
Thirty yards of board fence nine feet high.
Life to him seemed hollow, and existence but a burden.

톰은 하얀색 페인트가 담긴 양동이와 손잡이가 긴 붓을 들고 길가에 나타났다.
울타리를 살펴보자 모든 기쁨이 사라지고 우울한 마음이 생겨났다.
울타리는 길이가 30야드, 높이가 9피트였다.
삶이 공허하게 느껴졌고, 존재 자체가 짐 같았다. : 마크 트웨인 《톰 소여의 모험》

THE STRANGER came early in February,
one wintry day, through a biting wind year,
and a driving snow, the last snowfall of the year,
over the down, walking as it seemed from
Bramblehurst railway station, and carrying a little
black portmanteau in his thickly gloved hand.
He was wrapped up from head to foot, and the brim
of his soft felt hat hid every inch of his face
but the shiny tip of his nose.

THE STRANGER came early in February,
one wintry day, through a biting wind year,
and a driving snow, the last snowfall of the year,
over the down, walking as it seemed from
Bramblehurst railway station,
and carrying a little black portmanteau
in his thickly gloved hand. He was wrapped up
from head to foot, and the brim of his soft felt hat hid
every inch of his face but the shiny tip of his nose.

2월 초 어느 겨울날, 어떤 낯선 이가 매서운 바람과 휘몰아치는 눈을 뚫고,
브램블허스트 기차역에서 걸어왔다. 그는 두꺼운 장갑을 손에 끼고
작은 검은색 여행 가방을 들고 있었다. 그는 머리부터 발끝까지
감싸져 있었는데, 반짝이는 코끝을 제외하고는 부드러운 중절모가
그의 얼굴 전부를 가리고 있었다. : 허버트 조지 웰스 《투명인간》

Every step brought him nearer to London,
farther from his own sober inartistic life.
A light began to tremble on the horizon of his mind.
He was not so old—thirty-two. His temperament
might be said to be just at the point of maturity.
There were so many different moods and impressions
that he wished to express in verse. He felt them
within him. He tried to weigh his soul to see
if it was a poet's soul.

Every step brought him nearer to London,
farther from his own sober inartistic life.
A light began to tremble on the horizon of his mind.
He was not so old—thirty-two. His temperament
might be said to be just at the point of maturity.
There were so many different moods and impressions
that he wished to express in verse. He felt them
within him. He tried to weigh his soul to see
if it was a poet's soul.

걸음을 내디딜 때마다 그는 자신의 무미건조하고 비예술적인 삶에서 점점 멀어져, 런던에 더 가까워졌다. 마음의 지평선에서 빛이 떨리기 시작했다.
그는 서른두 살도 되지 않았다. 그의 기질은 바로 성숙기에 이르렀다고 할 수 있다.
그가 시로 표현하고 싶은 다양한 기분과 느낌이 너무나 많았다.
그는 내면에서 그것들을 느꼈다. 그는 그것이 시인의 영혼인지 알아보기 위해
자신의 영혼의 무게를 달아 보았다. : 제임스 조이스 《더블린 사람들 '작은 구름'》

"If only I could go with you," Wendy sighed.
"You see you can't fly," said Jane.
Of course in the end Wendy let them fly away together.
Our last glimpse of her shows her at the window,
watching them receding into the sky until
they were as small as stars.

"If only I could go with you," Wendy sighed.
"You see you can't fly," said Jane.
Of course in the end Wendy let them fly away together.
Our last glimpse of her shows her at the window,
watching them receding into the sky until
they were as small as stars.

"내가 너희들과 함께 갈 수만 있다면." 웬디가 한숨을 쉬었다.
"엄마는 날 수가 없잖아요." 제인이 말했다.
결국 웬디는 그들이 함께 날아가도록 허락했다.
웬디의 마지막 모습은 창가에 서서 하늘 저 멀리 날아가는
두 아이가 별처럼 작아질 때까지 지켜보고 있는 것이었다. : 제임스 배리 《피터팬》

A goal stood before Siddhartha, a single goal:
to become empty, empty of thirst, empty of wishing,
empty of dreams, empty of joy and sorrow.
Dead to himself, not to be a self any more,
to find tranquility with an emptied heart,
to be open to miracles in unselfish thoughts,
that was his goal.

A goal stood before Siddhartha, a single goal: to become empty,
empty of thirst, empty of wishing, empty of dreams, empty of joy
and sorrow. Dead to himself, not to be a self any more,
to find tranquility with an emptied heart, to be open to miracles
in unselfish thoughts, that was his goal.

싯다르타에게는 한 가지 목표밖에 없었다. 갈증으로부터 벗어나고, 꿈으로부터 벗어나고,
기쁨과 번뇌로부터 벗어나 자신을 비우는 것이었다. 자신을 남김없이 없애버리는 것,
자아로부터 벗어나 나 자신이 아닌 상태로 되는 것, 마음을 비워내고 평정심을 찾는 것,
자아를 버리고 경이로움에 마음을 여는 것, 그것이 그의 목표였다. : 헤르만 헤세 《싯다르타》

As the news of my arrival spread through the kingdom, it brought prodigious numbers of rich, idle, and curious people to see me; so that the villages were almost emptied; and great neglect of tillage and household affairs must have ensued, if his imperial majesty had not provided, by several proclamations and orders of state, against this inconveniency.

As the news of my arrival spread through the kingdom,
it brought prodigious numbers of rich, idle, and curious people
to see me; so that the villages were almost emptied;
and great neglect of tillage and household affairs
must have ensued, if his imperial majesty had not provided,
by several proclamations and orders of state,
against this inconveniency.

내가 도착했다는 소식이 왕국 전체에 퍼지자, 부자, 게으름뱅이, 호기심 많은 사람들이
나를 보기 위해 엄청나게 모여들었다. 그래서 마을이 거의 텅 비게 되었다.
만일 왕이 여러 선언과 법령으로 나를 보러 오는 일을 금지하지 않았다면,
나라의 농사와 집안일에 큰 피해가 있었을 것이다. : 조너선 스위프트 《걸리버 여행기》

Fifteen-year-old Jo was very tall, thin, and brown, and reminded one of a colt, for she never seemed to know what to do with her long limbs, which were very much in her way. She had a decided mouth, a comical nose, and sharp, gray eyes, which appeared to see everything, and were by turns fierce, funny, or thoughtful. Her long, thick hair was her one beauty, but it was usually bundled into a net, to be out of her way.

Fifteen-year-old Jo was very tall, thin, and brown, and reminded one of a colt, for she never seemed to know what to do with her long limbs, which were very much in her way. She had a decided mouth, a comical nose, and sharp, gray eyes, which appeared to see everything, and were by turns fierce, funny, or thoughtful. Her long, thick hair was her one beauty, but it was usually bundled into a net, to be out of her way.

열다섯 살인 조는 매우 큰 키에 마르고 피부는 가무잡잡했는데, 긴 팔다리를 어쩌할 줄 모르는 것이 꼭 망아지를 생각나게 했다. 그녀는 단호한 입, 웃기게 생긴 코를 가졌으며, 모든 것을 꿰뚫어 보는 듯한 날카로운 회색 눈에서는 분노나 장난기, 사려 깊은 생각이 드러났다. 숱이 많은 긴 머리는 그녀의 유일한 아름다움이었는데 대부분 머리 망으로 묶어두었다.

: 루이자 메이 올컷 《작은 아씨들》

It was now that I began sensibly to feel how much more happy this life I now led was, with all its miserable circumstances, than the wicked, cursed, abominable life I led all the past part of my days; and now I changed both my sorrows and my joys; my very desires altered, my affections changed their gusts, and my delights were perfectly new from what they were at my first coming, or, indeed, for the two years past.

It was now that I began sensibly to feel how much more happy this life I now led was, with all its miserable circumstances, than the wicked, cursed, abominable life I led all the past part of my days; and now I changed both my sorrows and my joys; my very desires altered, my affections changed their gusts, and my delights were perfectly new from what they were at my first coming, or, indeed, for the two years past.

나는 바로 지금의 모든 비참한 환경 속에서도, 내 삶이 과거에서 내가 살았던 사악하고 저주받고 가증스러웠던 삶보다 얼마나 더 행복한지 분명하게 느끼기 시작했다. 슬픔과 기쁨의 기준이 바뀌었고 욕망과 애정의 방향도 바뀌었다. 내 기쁨은 내가 이곳에 처음 왔을 때, 아니, 실제로 지난 2년 동안 느꼈던 감정으로부터 완전히 새로웠다. : 다니엘 디포 〈로빈슨 크루소〉

As the Cathedral clock struck two in the morning, Jean Valjean awoke. What woke him was that his bed was too good. It was nearly twenty years since he had slept in a bed, and, although he had not undressed, the sensation was too novel not to disturb his slumbers. He had slept more than four hours. His fatigue had passed away. He was accustomed not to devote many hours to repose. He opened his eyes and stared into the gloom which surrounded him; then he closed them again, with the intention of going to sleep once more.

As the Cathedral clock struck two in the morning, Jean Valjean awoke. What woke him was that his bed was too good. It was nearly twenty years since he had slept in a bed, and, although he had not undressed, the sensation was too novel not to disturb his slumbers. He had slept more than four hours. His fatigue had passed away. He was accustomed not to devote many hours to repose. He opened his eyes and stared into the gloom which surrounded him; then he closed them again, with the intention of going to sleep once more.

대성당 시계가 새벽 2시를 알리자, 장 발장은 잠에서 깼다. 그의 잠을 깨운 것은 침대가 너무 폭신했기 때문이었다. 침대에서 잠을 잔 건 거의 20년 만이었다. 비록 옷을 벗고 자지는 않았지만, 느낌이 너무 새로워 잠을 설쳤다. 그는 4시간 이상을 잤다. 피로가 풀렸다. 그는 긴 시간을 쉬는 데 익숙하지 않았다. 그는 눈을 뜨고 자신을 둘러싼 어둠을 응시하고는 좀 더 자려고 다시 눈을 감았다. : 빅토르 위고 《레 미제라블》

After the meal the friends had a long talk, or rather
the Town Mouse talked about her life in the city
while the Country Mouse listened. They then went
to bed in a cozy nest in the hedgerow and slept
in quiet and comfort until morning. In her sleep
the Country Mouse dreamed she was a Town Mouse
with all the luxuries and delights of city life
that her friend had described for her. So the next day
when the Town Mouse asked the Country Mouse
to go home with her to the city, she gladly said yes.

After the meal the friends had a long talk, or rather
the Town Mouse talked about her life in the city
while the Country Mouse listened. They then went
to bed in a cozy nest in the hedgerow and slept in quiet
and comfort until morning. In her sleep the Country Mouse
dreamed she was a Town Mouse with all the luxuries
and delights of city life that her friend had described for her.
So the next day when the Town Mouse asked the Country Mouse
to go home with her to the city, she gladly said yes.

식사를 마친 다음, 친구들은 긴 이야기를 나누었다.
더 정확히 말하자면 시골 쥐는 듣고 도시 쥐는 도시 생활에 대해 이야기했다.
그런 다음 그들은 산울타리의 아늑한 둥지에서 아침까지 편안하게 잠을 잤다.
시골 쥐는 친구가 이야기한, 화려하고 재미있는 도시 생활을 하는 꿈을 꾸었다.
그래서 다음 날 시골 쥐는 도시 쥐가 같이 도시로 가자고 하자 기꺼이 그러겠다고 대답했다.
: 이솝 《시골 쥐와 도시 쥐》

Towards two o'clock in the morning, the burning light reappeared, not less intense, about five miles to windward of the Abraham Lincoln. Notwithstanding the distance, and the noise of the wind and sea, one heard distinctly the loud strokes of the animal's tail, and even its panting breath. It seemed that, at the moment that the enormous narwhal had come to take breath at the surface of the water, the air was engulfed in its lungs, like the steam in the vast cylinders of a machine of two thousand horse-power.

Towards two o'clock in the morning, the burning light reappeared, not less intense, about five miles to windward of the Abraham Lincoln. Notwithstanding the distance, and the noise of the wind and sea, one heard distinctly the loud strokes of the animal's tail, and even its panting breath. It seemed that, at the moment that the enormous narwhal had come to take breath at the surface of the water, the air was engulfed in its lungs, like the steam in the vast cylinders of a machine of two thousand horse-power.

새벽 2시가 되자, '에이브러햄 링컨' 호에서 바람이 불어오는 방향으로 5마일 정도 떨어진 곳에서 강렬하게 타오르는 불빛이 다시 나타났다. 거리도 멀고, 바람 소리와 파도 소리로 시끄러웠지만 동물의 꼬리가 스치는 소리가 크게 들려왔고, 거친 숨소리까지 뚜렷하게 들렸다. 그 순간에 거대한 일각고래가 수면 위로 올라와 숨을 들이쉬자, 공기는 마치 2천 마력을 지닌 기계의 거대한 피스톤 속으로 빨려 들어가는 수증기 같았다. : 쥘 베른 《해저 2만리》

Now he was a sturdy straw-haired man of thirty with a rather hard mouth and a supercilious manner. Two shining arrogant eyes had established dominance over his face and gave him the appearance of always leaning aggressively forward. Not even the effeminate swank of his riding clothes could hide the enormous power of that body—he seemed to fill those glistening boots until he strained the top lacing, and you could see a great pack of muscle shifting when his shoulder moved under his thin coat.

Now he was a sturdy straw-haired man of thirty with a rather hard mouth and a supercilious manner. Two shining arrogant eyes had established dominance over his face and gave him the appearance of always leaning aggressively forward. Not even the effeminate swank of his riding clothes could hide the enormous power of that body—he seemed to fill those glistening boots until he strained the top lacing, and you could see a great pack of muscle shifting when his shoulder moved under his thin coat.

이제 그는 밀짚 색깔의 머리카락에 다소 무뚝뚝하게 생긴 입과 거만한 태도를 가진 서른 살의 건장한 남자였다. 거만한 눈빛이 그의 얼굴을 지배하고 있어 항상 몸을 앞으로 기울여 공격적인 태도를 취하는 것 같았다. 여성스러운 승마복조차도 그의 육체에서 나오는 엄청난 힘을 숨길 수 없었다. 그의 번쩍이는 장화는 맨 위쪽 끈이 팽팽해질 때까지 꽉 채워져 있었다. 그의 어깨가 움직일 때마다, 얇은 상의 아래로 튼튼한 근육이 움직이는 것이 보였다.
: 스콧 피츠제럴드 《위대한 개츠비》

Almost every criminal is subject to a failure of will and reasoning power by a childish and phenomenal heedlessness, at the very instant when prudence and caution are most essential. It was his conviction that this eclipse of reason and failure of will power attacked a man like a disease, developed gradually and reached its highest point just before the perpetration of the crime, continued with equal violence at the moment of the crime and for longer or shorter time after, according to the individual case, and then passed off like any other disease.

Almost every criminal is subject to a failure of will and reasoning power by a childish and phenomenal heedlessness, at the very instant when prudence and caution are most essential. It was his conviction that this eclipse of reason and failure of will power attacked a man like a disease, developed gradually and reached its highest point just before the perpetration of the crime, continued with equal violence at the moment of the crime and for longer or shorter time after, according to the individual case, and then passed off like any other disease.

거의 모든 범죄자들은 신중함과 주의력이 가장 필요한 바로 그 순간, 유치하고 경이적인 경솔함으로 인해 의지와 이성적 사고능력이 떨어진다. 그의 신념은 이성이 나약해지고 의지력이 꺾이는 것은 질병처럼 사람을 덮치고, 점점 발전해 범행 직전에 최고조에 달하고 개인에 따라 범죄 당시 또는 그 이후에 길거나 짧게 유지되다가 다른 질병처럼 사라진다는 것이다. : 표도르 도스토옙스키 《죄와 벌》

100일 간의 완주를 기념하며 영어 필기체로 수료증을 멋지게 완성해보세요.

Certificate of Completion

100 days of English Cursive Handwriting Miracle Workbook

Congratulations!

Name _____

Date of Birth _____

Address _____

The date of Completion _____

Signature _____